Small Books on Great Gardens

MAJORELLE

A Moroccan Oasis

Madison Cox and Pierre Bergé

Photography by Claire de Virieu

Contents

Majorelle

by Pierre Bergé

When we arrived in Marrekesh the first time, Yves Saint Laurent and I were, like everyone else, utterly seduced by the beauty and magic of the surrounding country. About the town, nothing remained to be said or written, but what we did not suspect was that we would fall in love with a small, mysterious garden, painted in the colors of Henri Matisse and secluded in a bamboo forest, all silence, deeply sheltered from both noise and wind. This was the Majorelle Garden. Years later, quite by chance, we came into possession of this jewel and set about saving it. Aided by Bill Willis and Jacques Granges, we decided to bring life back to the house built next to the garden. We gave it a beautiful name, taken from the title of a book by Eugène Dabit: Villa Oasis.

For captions of previous illustrations, see page 80. *Opposite*: The extraordinary forms of many plants cast dramatic shadows not only on other plants, but even across their own leaves. *Overleaf*: Majorelle originally painted the square pool and fountain and the studio building this vivid blue in the early 1930s as a backdrop to his exotic plant collection.

11

Two approaches to the studio building. *Right*, cacti and other plants grow cheek by jowl along the raised path. *Opposite*, clad in *Bougainvillea* and Cape honeysuckle or *Tecomaria capensis*, the pergola links the studio building seen at one end with the aloe walk located at the far corner of the garden.
Overleaf: Viewed from above, the garden path system meanders partially hidden. The sense of mystery and discovery is heightened by continuous path-level changes and succeeding areas of bright light and dark shadow.

A garden open to the public is unlike any other kind of garden. Its mystery springs not from secret corners, which are few, but rather from the whole arrangement. Paths are relatively wide, the better to help visitors find their way. Benches provide moments of rest, and thus an opportunity to discover views, perspectives, or leafy, floral masses. The plants impose a sense of peace.

Then, almost insidiously, they grow stranger, even puzzling.

Among the gardens I know, the one that most completely offers such an experience was designed and planted by Jacques Majorelle in Morocco. Close by Medina, an ordinary street filled with pushcart merchants selling oranges and lemons gives access to a broad path of beaten earth lined with pink laurel and bordered by adobe walls. This leads to a blue-brick

entrance hung with a green-painted wooden door, which opens on to the garden.

Here we are greeted first by groves of bamboo. They come as a surprise in this environment, and the water surrounding them looks quite odd under the African sun. Some of the trees, imported from Malaysia, stand in clumps, so that their green-striped yellow stalks form

a kind of palisade. The walkways are paved in simple concrete dyed red; the chamaerops palms are blue, the glaucous yuccas almost black; and the dragon trees a gleaming presence. Bougainvillea mount to the challenge of the pritchardias (Loulou palms), while water lilies spread wide across the surfaces of the fountains. Papyruses, both Egyptian and alternifoliate varieties, sway back and forth, leaving the caladiums and philodendrons to shelter the frogs and water turtles.

Opposite: view from the raised pergola adjacent to the painting studio, the square pool is linked with the long water rill, which recedes into the far reaches of the garden. Majorelle incorporated both water features characteristic of Islamic gardens and transformed them as garden elements by the use of the strong blue paint, seen also, *right*, in a more open design.

Then, suddenly, at the turn of the path, we come upon the house—the house of Jacques Majorelle. It is painted blue; a strong, hard blue. Blazing under the sun like an unfurled flag, it is bordered by a turquoise pergola. The window frames are yellow. A fountain breaks the silence. In the distance, beyond a channel of water, stands a Moroccan kiosk in the midst of *moucharabies.* Now it becomes clear that we are at the home of a painter, in a garden designed, composed, and colored like a painting. Immediately one thinks of Henri Matisse, for we are indeed at the very center of a Matisse, soaked in color—chilly greens, acid yellows, and hot blues. Everything here conjures up painting, and not least among the many virtues of Jacques Majorelle is the fact that he succumbed to the spell of this country, lived here, and created this place as a complete ensemble.

Today Majorelle has long been dead and Matisse as well. Only a few canvases bear witness to the latter's Moroccan period. But in Marrekesh, tucked away by itself, a small, rare garden celebrates, in every season, the strange marriage of painting and nature.

The Majorelle Garden

by Madison Cox

The Majorelle Garden, located in the southern Moroccan desert oasis of Marrekesh, is one of this century's most enchanting, even mystical, garden experiences. Created over the course of nearly forty years, the garden complex is a labyrinth composed of bisecting pathways and inter-connected levels, Moorish and Art Deco-inspired structures, and bold palettes, all assembled among a vast, opulent array of exotic plants and trees collected from the far reaches of the world. Conceived as a walled inner sanctum and laboratory by French-born painter Jacques Majorelle, the garden is a place of individual expression and great power rarely seen in contemporary garden design.

Straddling the northwestern edge of the African continent and perched between the Atlantic Ocean and

Opposite: Majorelle placed large terra-cotta pots throughout the garden, many of which are painted bright yellows, greens, and blues. Here an olive jar, planted with zonale pelargoniums, marks a gate leading to another part of the garden.

the Mediterranean Sea, Morocco has been in the unique position of witnessing and absorbing myriad cultural and political influences over the centuries from Roman, Phoenician, Moorish, and European occupation. A country rich in topographical variety, Morocco is composed of vast beach-front coastlines, snow-capped mountain chains, cedar and pine forests, rich agricultural valleys of citrus and olive groves, and arid desert plains. The country has inspired and seduced such diverse writers as Pierre Loti, Edith Wharton, and Paul Bowles with its heady and colorfully complex tableaux. A multifarious culture that permeates, captures, and mesmerizes, Morocco is an extremely powerful place that captivates the mind and soul. It is that multilayered and hugely exotic cultural atmosphere that caught the imagination and vision of Jacques Majorelle in the early years of the twentieth century.

The only son of Louis Majorelle, the celebrated furniture-maker and founder of the *School of Nancy*, Jacques Majorelle was born in 1886 into the center of the creative artistic rebellion that came to be known as the French Art Nouveau movement. Nancy, the small, jewel-like capital of Lorraine in northeastern France, was renowned for its rich heritage in all forms of the arts, from architecture and painting to the decorative arts. Like his co-founder Emile Gallé, Louis Majorelle was a

Opposite: Detail of the training pink-flowering geranium, which has become leggy with age. The garden has relatively few bright flowers, relying instead on half-hidden spots of color that seem to pop out against the rich variations of greens.
Above: The doorway into the Museum of Islamic Art is shaded by the tangled massed profusion of plants and vines that adds to the mystery of the garden.

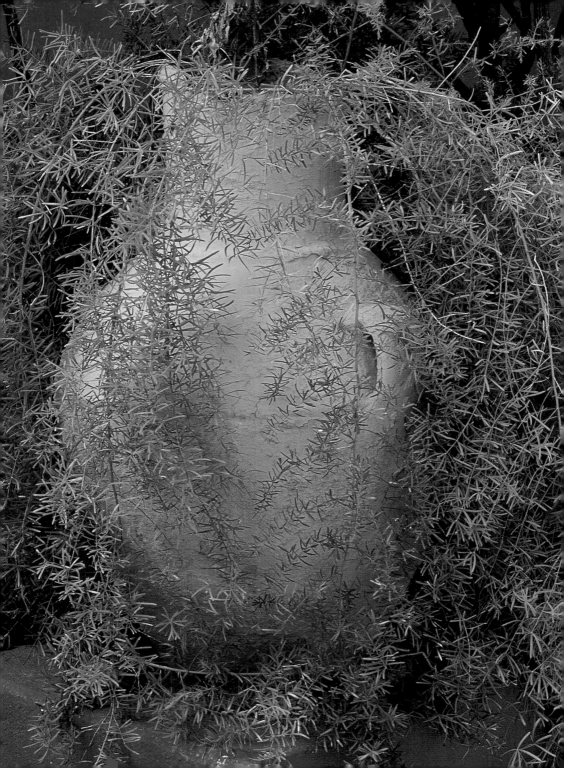

Previous pages, left:
Potted geraniums and
Kalanchoe fedtschenkoi
ring the gigantic
Beaucarnea recurvata, the
Ponytail or Bottle Palm,
which is commonly seen
only as a house plant.
Previous pages, right:
Planted throughout the
garden, the Sprenger
asparagus is mistakenly
called a fern and does well
in containers, in bright
sun, as well as in semi-
shade.
Opposite: Framing the
pergola entrance on the
left are the trumpet-like,
pendulous flowers of the
datura or *Brugmansia
candida*, which is native to
Peru. It is highly fragrant
in early evening, when the
garden comes alive as the
varied scents mingle and
the pale flowering plants
begin to glow with the
fading sun.

symbolist who revolted against the pastiche and
mediocrity that came to represent the decorative arts in
the second half of the nineteenth century. Drawing
inspiration from the natural world, the School of Nancy,
like its English counterpart the Arts and Crafts
movement, rooted its designs on the forms found in
nature. Great importance was placed on the study of
plant forms and their structures, which in turn would
have a profound influence for Majorelle's son. For
Jacques Majorelle, this artistically based childhood was to
play a crucial role in his formation as an artist, as well as
his enduring fascination with nature and plant forms.

After following the prerequisite classical Beaux-Arts
training as a painter in Parisian art academies,
including the celebrated Academie Julian, Majorelle
continued his education with extensive travel in Spain,
Italy, Greece, and Egypt, where he was to live for nearly
four years. During these travels Majorelle discovered the
fascination for foreign, mysterious lands held by
previous generations of artists and poets. Yet it was not
the sensual, luxuriant qualities of the distant countries
that attracted Majorelle—as it had for Delacroix or
Maxime du Camp—but rather the realism of their
existing cultural characteristics and their alien and
fierce individualism. In 1917, suffering from poor
health that resulted in an exemption from military

Above: One of countless Chinese hibiscus contributing
to the extraordinary palette of the gardens.
Opposite: A study in contrasts as spiky leaves
and rigid cacti provide a background, and shade,
for a more vulnerable looking neighbor.

Opposite: The blue-painted backdrop of the buildings seems to recede, enhancing the dramatic shapes of the vegetation. Majorelle likened his choice of the vivid blue to that of a jeweler's black velvet tray, which is the best method for displaying fine stones and pearls. *Overleaf*: The strong rectilinear lines of the buildings and pathways are softened by the lush, verdant vegetation. Created as a retreat from the heat and blinding sun, the Majorelle Garden has many leafy, light-dappled areas unfolding one unto the other.

service in World War I, the painter took the advice of a close family friend, the influential Resident-General of France in Morocco, General Lyautey, and visited Morocco. This restorative sojourn proved so successful that Majorelle remained in his adopted country until his death in 1962.

General Lyautey was an unmatched personality in the history of modern Morocco, and one who had great respect for the country's artistic traditions. Controlled by France as an occupied country, Morocco in the early decades of this century was a place of great transition, of converging modern and ancient worlds and European influences colliding with antique traditions. Travel between the cities was dangerous, and many parts of the country were inaccessible, if not uncharted. Fiefdoms, mountainous Berber tribes, and an expanding French population combined to make a place of great flux. Edith Wharton, the American writer and garden enthusiast, received an invitation from General Lyautey the same year as Majorelle; one result of her visit was the publication of her travel essay, *In Morocco*. She recounts the harsh realities of trekking from one city to the next, while her descriptions of the unspoiled beauty contained in this country are spellbinding. Upon arrival in the medieval city of Marrekesh she wrote:

"Outspread below lies the oasis-city of the south, flat

and vast as the great nomad camp it really is, its low roofs extending on all sides to a belt of blue palms ringed with desert. Only two or three minarets and a few noblemen's houses among gardens break the general flatness; but they are hardly noticeable, so irresistibly is the eye drawn towards two dominant objects--the white wall of the Atlas and the red tower of the Koutoubya."

Situated on a flat valley between the sand castle-like peaks of the Djebliets hills to the north and the soaring, snow-covered Atlas Mountains to the south, Marrekesh is an oasis of palm forests amid the dried, red-earth terrain. Surrounded by a green band cultivated for centuries with olive, almond, and citrus groves, the city is a paradise found for travelers as plentiful mountain water runoff transformed the arid landscape. Marrekesh is often referred to as the "rose-hued city" due to the forbidding red mud defense ramparts that ring the oldest sections, while the air is sometimes clouded with winds from the Sahara desert that fill the atmosphere with a pinkish dust. It is a mesmerizing place, and it captivated Jacques Majorelle from the moment he arrived.

Before permanently settling in Marrekesh, Majorelle used the city as a base for a number of years for excursions as far south into the African continent as the Ivory Coast. Numerous treks throughout Morocco

Opposite: From above the variety and density of planting are apparent, as are such recurring elements as repetition of strong verticals and diagonals and mingled textures.
Overleaf: At each vantage point endless series of vignettes unfold, adding to the garden's vibrancy and imbuing the enclosed landscape with a kinetic energy. The garden is about receding planes of shade and shadow that increase the sense of oasis or retreat from the blinding hot sun outside the walled complex.

39

exposed the painter to the rich variety of cultures, but none as importantly as his trips into the unknown territories of the Atlas Mountains, which separate the city from the Sahara to the southwest. In these high altitudes lived the Berber tribes in villages of square, tower-like structures amid landscapes almost completely devoid of vegetation. On his expeditions to paint and draw these mountain dwellers Majorelle was struck by their tradition of painting window frames and parts of facades with a vivid cobalt hue known today in Morocco as *"Bleu Majorelle."* By observing and recording diverse aspects of Moroccan culture, Majorelle became one of its leading proponents and resurrected many of the ancient motifs and techniques found in local decorative arts by championing their use to the building colonialists. Traces still exist in Marrekesh of Majorelle's work from the mid-twenties, the most notable example being the Mamounia Hotel, with its painted ceilings, odd lots of furniture, and a stuccoed wall map of the region.

It wasn't until 1924 that the painter purchased a plot outside the walled city on the edge of the sand-swept palm forest near the European quarter. Here Majorelle constructed his personal residence as well as a separate tower resembling those of the Berbers in the mountains. By 1931 Majorelle had added a large, cube-shaped, concrete painting studio inspired by French

Previous pages: Sunlight is highly filtered through the superimposed layers of tall trees and palms, climbing vines, and overgrown shrubs, and is dappled throughout the garden creating the tranquil, almost refreshing, atmosphere that attracts thousands of visitors annually.

Another view, *opposite*, of the square pool in late summer, when the water surface is covered with flowering water lilies, *above*. The brightly colored pots add a sense of rhythm and symmetry to the otherwise jungle-like atmosphere.

45

Opposite: The Majorelle Garden has become home to numerous species of birds and such aquatic creatures as bullfrogs, goldfish, and turtles, which were originally introduced to the area by Majorelle himself.

architect Robert Mallet-Stevens, then in vogue in Europe. With cantilevered roofs projecting from the façades to provide shade from the hot sun, and with no exterior decoration, the studio was in complete contrast to the style of the Moroccan-themed villa he erected and decorated for himself and his wife. Concurrent with the construction of the buildings, imposing compact earth walls were put up to contain them, and within this area the garden was laid out.

Although the Majorelle Garden as we know it today is roughly half the size it was during the painter's life, the area open to the public is the core of his garden, and contains his painting studio, the heart of the complex. Measuring less than an acre overall, the walled compound still evokes the atmosphere Majorelle created over half a century ago. On leaving the dusty and bustling wide avenue that defines one edge of the complex, one immediately senses relief and privilege upon entering the garden through its green gate. Here languid tranquillity is touched with an element of hesitation, and surprise reigns. The key concept is respite from the hot and parched elements of the outer world, so the garden is luxuriant, awash in a strange, almost phantasmagorical dappled light that increases the sensation of bizarre peacefulness. This is a place of strong emotions that counterbalance the harsh exterior

The arrow-shaped leaves of the caladiums grow in both the full sun pools, *right*, and the shady rill, *opposite*, that leads to the studio building. Plants are often grown throughout the garden, unifying the various spaces.
Overleaf: The long water rill links the Moroccan pavilion with the painting studio. One of the few truly Moroccan structures in the garden, the pavilion is nestled in the leafy confines of bamboo, another plant imported by Majorelle. Tall clumps of papyrus, or *Cyperus papyrus*, and caladiums dot the center of the water channel, while Mexican fan palms, or *Washingtonia robusta*, yuccas, and cacti line the sides.

realities; contained within its walls are the sounds of foliage rattling, birds chirping, frogs croaking, fountains playing, and people talking in hushed voices, all of which contribute to the garden's magical ambiance.

Majorelle incorporated a great number of old Moroccan agricultural techniques that he had noticed on his wandering. One important feature that

conditioned the general layout was dividing the garden into small areas contained within very low concrete curbs, which in turn created raised pedestrian walks averaging about a foot high. This system enabled the enclosed planted areas to be irrigated by means of flooding, which conserves water while giving the viewer the unique impression of walking above the plantings in some cases, and walking within the masses of vegetation in others. There is no formal composition to the layout

Opposite: Many of the plants grow within dense arrangements of contrasting varieties, while others, such as this agave, are placed as individual specimens, often alone in grass or periwinkle beds. *Overleaf*: The garden's discerning qualities lie in its ability to force the viewer to slow down and look. It is within the subtle treatment of such elements as the contrasting verticals and sharp diagonals on the left or the ephemeral and delicate flowering cacti on the right that the garden distinguishes itself.

of the pathways, which rise and fall by means of brick or tile steps, further increasing the sensation of greater space within this labyrinth. Smaller secondary pathways, many used by the gardeners to access thickly planted areas, encircle masses of vegetation or simply end at the trunk of a palm. This haphazard assemblage adds to the individualism of the place and gives it a unique sense of sequence.

By 1931 the new garden was completely transformed by Majorelle when he painted the entire exterior studio structure in the same vivid blue he had seen in the high Atlas Mountains. The courageous use of color in architectural design has become relatively familiar in recent years, but Majorelle's use of blue was very novel for that era, and both enlivened the garden and acted as a strong backdrop to his expanding plant collection. This bold stroke was on a far greater scale than ever applied before and revolutionized the way in which gardens were to be viewed. Since his death and increased public awareness and access to the garden, the use of Majorelle blue in Marrekesh has entered into the local architectural vocabulary as well as becoming synonymous with the garden itself.

The studio facade did not remain the only surface to be painted blue, and over time the fountains, water rills, pond-viewing platform, garden pots, pergolas,

walkway curbs, and gates were all treated with the vivid hue. The blue of Majorelle was not the only color employed by the artist, as he incorporated the rich, red pigment characteristic of Marrekesh on pot surfaces and into the smooth concrete walkways and raised planting beds. Since the restoration the new owners, Yves Saint Laurent and Pierre Bergé, have continued this tradition, including the incorporation of a rich yet pale yellow into the garden palette.

Water, a primary element in all Islamic gardens and especially in the hot, dry climate of Marrekesh, was used throughout the garden, again continuing the use of traditional elements. An elaborate system of small canals connect the various planted areas and infuse the garden with its sight and sound. A long rill with a tile pavilion at one end recalls faded images of Islam, while other water features include a square tank with a splashing fountain and a large basin containing water lilies and lotus. The audible aspects of water enhance the luxuriant qualities of the garden, as well as producing an atmosphere that is slightly humid, and hence cooler.

Perhaps no greater image of the garden comes to mind than the vast plant collection contained within. Like fellow artist Claude Monet, Majorelle was to become one of the most important plant collectors of his

time, and his garden became the backdrop for his canvases. Similar to Monet in his vast quest for new plants, Majorelle financed plant expeditions, imported rare varieties, and corresponded with other collectors and botanical gardens around the world. Cacti imported from the American Southwest, palms shipped from the South Pacific, succulents from South Africa, and water lilies and lotus collected in Asia are all examples of Majorelle's intense interest in amassing an important array of plants.

The garden is not about color harmonies in the European sense. There are no mixed borders, single-theme color compositions, or even blocks of contrasting hues, but rather an overpowering abundance of vegetal shapes and forms. The contrasting effects of light and shadow are repeatedly played against each other as a darkened area opens onto a sunlit one, which in turn reveals other forbiddingly shadowy paths. Soaring palms, dragon trees, jacarandas, and towering cypress all cast shadows onto the lower arched banana fronds, bamboo, palmetto mounds, *Cycas revoluta*, or sago palms, which forge dense blocks of vegetation. Teeming vines such as the vividly hued magenta or purple bougainvillea or plumbago enshroud vertical surfaces as they climb bowers, pergolas, walls, or tree trunks in a seemingly wild fashion.

61

Opposite: The columns of this pergola echo the strong verticals of the Mexican fan palms and other trees, and also support a mix of flowering vines.

Plant structures define the garden as silhouettes are boldly juxtaposed and united creating varying areas of intense atmosphere. Dense groves of bamboo, over twenty different varieties, are thickly planted, creating a dappled, if not hauntingly shadowed walk, while agaves now towering nine feet in height and planted in a straight row along one walk project menacingly onto the pathway, obliging the passer-by to proceed with extreme care. Giant euphorbias, jade trees, echeverias, pincushion-shaped barrel cactus, and spiky aloes were all chosen for their strong, graphic shapes and silhouettes, which increase the surrealistic sense of the place. While the garden is neither soft nor pastoral it remains a quiet, ghostly refuge and in direct contrast to the outside world.

There are times during the warmer months of the year when the scorching and blinding sun reduces the blue plant to traced lines against the black velvet-like background. In winter, when the skies are gray and the air damp with moisture, the varying gray-greens of the plants meld with the painted blue watery surfaces and become ethereal, creating an underwater effect in the garden, again underlining the garden's mysterious qualities. The garden changes most dramatically in the late afternoon, when the light softens and the plant forms begin to merge into each other. The bright hues

Parts of the garden seem almost tame, *above*,
when compared to the more wild corners, *opposite*.
But in fact Majorelle's major concerns–variety, color,
and integration–are found throughout the garden.

recede, the pale flowers of the datura and yellow water lilies emerge, creating a cloud-like airiness. Constantly in a state of flux, the garden captures the harsh sunlight and transforms it into a tamed element that defies any known example. Majorelle's greatest work of art is his garden, a composition that continues to capture, mesmerize, and enrapture the visiting public.

Opposite: Majorelle was instrumental in preserving such Moroccan crafts as carved plaster, which he often incorporated into his various projects. Along the entrance walk to the Museum of Islamic Arts, large panels of decorative plaster work frame the building's small windows. *Left*: Delicate touches abound, and serve as nuance in otherwise bold, dramatic compositions.

71

Garden Plan
and Visiting
Information

Majorelle is open to the public
every day of the year.

Summer visiting hours are
from 8:00 a.m. to 12 noon,
and from 3:00 p.m. to 7:00 p.m.
Winter visiting hours are
from 8:00 a.m. to 12 noon,
and from 2:00 p.m. to 5:00 p.m.

For further information write:
Majorelle Garden
Avenue Yacoub el Mansour
Marrekesh, Morocco

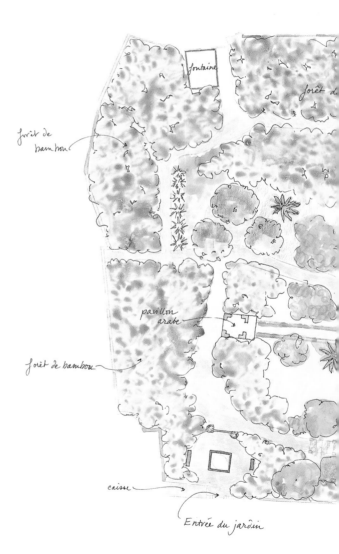

Majorelle Garden
Marrekesh

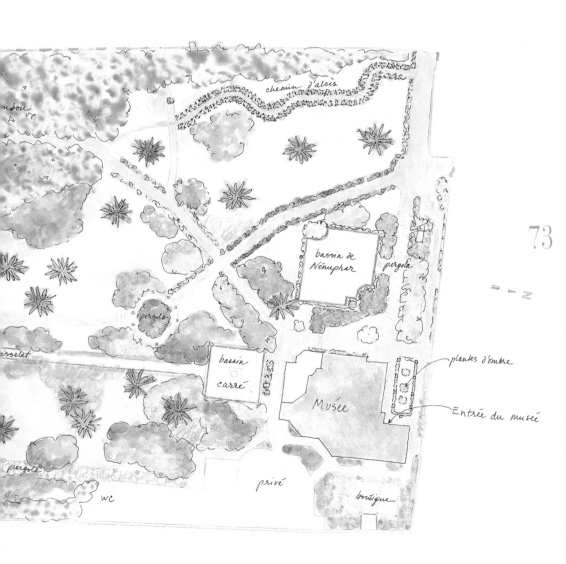

chemin d'aloès

bassin de Nénuphar

pergola

pergola

bassin carré

Musée

plantes d'ombre

Entrée du musée

isselet

pergola

wc

privé

boutique

Previous pages: Jacques Majorelle, in 1921 painting a scene of the old town of Marrekesh. *Opposite:* The ground floor salon of Majorelle's Villa Bou Saf-Saf in Marrekesh with a splendid polychrome Islamic interior that is quite similar to that built at the nearby Hotel Mamounia in 1921. *Above:* The elegantly dressed artist on his terrace in 1950. European clothes are accented by a colourful arabic skullcap. *Below:* Dates in Marrekesh. 1924. Oil on canvas. Private collection. This lush painting converys the natural richness of a Moroccan oasis.

Above: The Date Souk in Marrekesh. Oil on canvas. Private collection.
Below: A Street in a Marrekesh Souk. Oil on canvas. Private collection.
Opposite: Morocco via Marseilles. 1926. Lithograph. Private collection. In the 1920s, Morocco became a winter paradise, particularly for the French, who travelled there on the Paris-Lyon-Méditeranée a line to enjoy the splendid climate and the delights of the Orient. Majorelle enjoyed receving visitors in his lovely house and magnificent gardens.

Page 1: The saber-like fronds of the *Agave franzosinii* are characteristic of the exotic plants that Jacques Majorelle imported from the far reaches of the globe.

Pages 2-3: The spiky variegated foliage of the agave is in striking contrast with the lush tumbling vegetation of the vines behind. Majorelle often employed the garden backdrop as a setting for his figurative paintings.

Pages 4-5: Some of the oldest cacti are located nearest the artist's studio and include, from left to right, *Echinocactus sp.*, *Pachycereus calvus*, and *Espostoa cephalum*, which are inter-planted with *Agave angustifolia* and *A. sisalana*, all of which originate in Mexico and Central America.

Page 6: The tall crinkled leaves of the *Kalanchoe baharensis* are in stark contrast with the pale blue pergola of Majorelle's painting studio.

Page 8: The wrought-iron window grill was painted yellow by Yves Saint Laurent during the restoration of Jacques Majorelle's painting studio, which now houses the Museum of Islamic Art.

First published in the United Kingdom in 1999 by Thames & Hudson Ltd, 181A High Holborn, London WC1V 7QX

British Library Cataloguing-in-Publication Data
A catalogue record for this book is available from the British Library

ISBN 0-500-01976-2

Printed and bound in Italy

Series editor Gabrielle Van Zuylen
Designed by Marc Walter / Bela Vista